Writing Springboards

Lottie Kent

springboards

My

Year 6

HOPSCOTCH EDUCATIONAL PUBLISHING

Published by
Hopscotch Educational Publishing Ltd,
Unit 2, The Old Brushworks, 56 Pickwick Road,
Corsham, Wiltshire SN13 9BX
Tel: 01249 701701

© 2004 Hopscotch Educational Publishing

Written by Lottie Kent
Series design by Blade Communications
Illustrated by Lottie Kent
Printed by cle-print

ISBN 1-904307-66-3

Contents

Introduction

About the series

Writing Springboards is an innovative series of books aimed at developing and enriching the writing skills of children at Key Stage 2. The activities are matched to the National Literacy Strategy's *Framework for Teaching* for Years 3 to 6 but the activities could easily be used with older or younger children.

There are four books in the series: Year 3, Year 4, Year 5 and Year 6.

Each book aims to:
- support teachers by providing a wealth of interesting ideas for writing lessons;
- reduce teachers' preparation time through the provision of photocopiable resources;
- stimulate children's interest and enjoyment in writing;
- develop and enhance children's writing skills through stimulating and purposeful activities that are fun to do.

Written and illustrated by a practising teacher, the activities have been trialled in schools with outstanding success. The ideas are fresh and exciting and guidance is provided to enable teachers to use the same activity in a variety of different ways.

About each book

Each book contains 15 units of work, specifically written to cover the range of text level work outlined in the *Literacy Framework* for each year group. Where appropriate to the activity, there are also some sentence level objectives included. The activities can be used throughout the school year, enabling the teacher to focus on developing appropriate skills in fiction, poetry and non-fiction writing for each term.

Each unit consists of four photocopiable sheets plus teacher's notes that provide lots of practical ideas and suggestions for how the sheets can be used.

The three photocopiable activity sheets can be used for differentiated tasks for specific children or groups during a lesson, or within a series of literacy lessons where the children may work as a whole class, in groups or individually. Where particular children need support, the sheets can be used to prepare them for a writing activity, giving them more confidence to contribute their ideas. They are also an ideal way to motivate the more reluctant writers in a class. The activities will inspire children's creativity and add sparkle to any lesson!

The fourth photocopiable sheet contains just the main illustration and this can be used in a variety of ways:
- as a stimulus for writing assessment;
- for generating the teacher's own questions as an introduction to the writing task;
- as a starting point for a writing activity in a different genre;
- to use in discussion, developing the children's skills in speaking and listening;
- for the teacher to make it into a word bank to support specific children;
- for SEN support – working on a child's particular literacy targets

At the back of the book are some extra sheets that can be used to support any of the units.

Response partners sheet
This can be used to encourage children to work with others to evaluate their work and make decisions about possible improvements to their writing.

Self-assessment sheet
This can be used to help focus the writer on assessing the key aspects of their writing and evaluate their success.

Writing targets sheet
This can be used to help pupils to concentrate on areas for improvement.

Publishing and display ideas sheets
These sheets can be used by both the teacher and the children themselves to provide them with lots of exciting ideas for publishing and displaying their writing.

Unit 1 – The rose

Learning objectives

- To prepare a short section of story as a script (Term 1, T9).
- To develop use of Shakespearean style language (Term 1, T6).
- To create suitable characters for a play.

Ideas for using the activity sheets

Page 6: The Rose

- Look at the setting for the scene. Discuss how this could be planned as production notes for a play and how it would include the set design, lighting and sound. Ask the children to work in pairs to write down the production notes for the scene. Share their ideas – have they included enough/too much detail?
- Look at examples of play scenes and discuss how they build up. Are all the characters on stage at the beginning/end of the scene? The children could work in small groups planning stage directions and lines for the start of the scene. They could perform it to the class.
- Look at the plot from a Shakespearean play. Discuss how it develops. The children could then work in small groups, planning the plot for this play. What could be happening? What is the significance of the rose? Who are the main characters? Once completed, ask the groups to share their ideas with the class. Could their plans be used to write a Shakespearean play?

Page 7: The Rose – conversation

- Make a collection of words and phrases that Shakespeare used. Can the children work out a rough translation? Can they make up their own words and phrases? Ask the children to work in pairs to invent their own words/phrases that could be used. Tell them to make up lines for the two characters including their own invented words. They could perform the lines - can others work out what they're trying to say?
- Use volunteers to take on the role of each character and use hot seating to find out what sort of characters they are. Make a list of characteristics for both characters. Who do they think is the good/bad character? Why have they made these choices? Discuss stereotypes. The children could use the character profiles to complete the sheet.
- As a whole class, make up a basic conversation between the characters. Look at the different effects in language that Shakespeare used; for example, personification, alliteration, metaphors, similes and so on. The children could work in pairs, developing the basic lines using the listed effects. Share their favourite lines with the class – have they retained the basic meaning?

Page 8: The Rose scene

- The children could use the lines created previously and work in groups of four to build up the script for the whole scene, including stage directions, production notes and props. They can adapt their ideas as it progresses, using suggestions from the group. They could perform the finished piece to another group.
- Ask the children to develop their ideas in the next scene of the play. Which other characters will they introduce? Ask them to write and practise the new scene as a small group and share the performance with the rest of the class.
- In pairs, the children could each take on the role of a character. They could make up lines for the scene, practising their performance. Provide props for the children to use and ask for volunteers to perform to the class.

The rose

Make notes around the picture.

Where is it set?

When is it?

Who is he?

Why is he there?

Describe his character.

What is the importance of the rose?

What has happened before?

Who is she?

Why is she there?

What is she thinking?

Describe her character.

What will happen next?

The rose – conversation

Write what each character would say.

Make a collection of Shakespearean words and phrases to use.

The rose scene

What are they talking about?

Names?

Are there pauses?

How are they speaking?

How are they feeling?

Are there any actions?

Write out the scene shown. Use the prompts to help.

Setting:

Characters:

Scene:

....

....

....

....

....

....

....

....

....

....

Unit 2 – Pirate treasure

Learning objectives

- To write in the style of classic fiction.
- To manipulate narrative perspective (Term 1, T6).
- To plan aspects of a story quickly and effectively (Term 1, T7).

Ideas for using the activity sheets

Page 11: Pirate treasure

- Ask the children to research the lifestyle of a pirate. They could use this information to build up a class list of the key aspects to consider when completing the sheet.
- Look at extracts from classic pirate stories. What is special about how they are written? Which aspects do they like about the style used? They could complete the planning sheet and use this to write the scene in the style of a classic author.
- Discuss how the scene could be written in a modern setting. What could the treasure be? What type of boat could they be on? They could complete the plans in pairs and share their finished plans with the class.

Page 12: Different narrators

- Find out about famous pirates, recording their characteristics and reasons for fame. The children could write the scene using a famous pirate as one of the two characters. They need to give clues as to the identity of the pirate without actually naming him. Share the finished pieces – can the others guess who it is? Was it harder to give clues when writing with the pirate as narrator?
- Make a collection of phrases used by pirates. What do they mean? Display a list of them with translations. Ask the children to complete the sheet, trying to use as many of the phrases in appropriate places as they can. Read out the finished pieces and discuss their use of pirate language.
- Hot seat a volunteer in the role of the pirate. The children could ask questions about the scene and how the pirate is feeling. Record their responses and use them in a written description. The children could work in small groups to hot seat each other in the role of the person hiding.

Page 13: Pirate treasure plan

- Look at film or television dramas based on pirate stories. Discuss how aspects such as settings, narrator, dialogue and so on would differ from those in a written version. Complete the plan as a whole class and ask the children to choose part of the plan to write as a script for a film version. The script could be used to write a scene to be acted out in small groups.
- Look at examples of stories that have two narrators. Discuss how this could work with this story. Plan the story as a class and use it over a series of lessons, writing different parts and focusing on the use of two narrators.
- The children could use the completed plan to write a series of diary entries made by one of the two characters shown. Discuss how this will differ from a story. Can they write it in the style of a classic author? Publish their finished work as a diary and display it for other children to read.

Pirate treasure

Make notes around the picture.

Who is hiding?

When is it?

Why is he/she hiding?

How does he/she feel?

Where has the treasure come from?

What is in the small box?

Where is it set?

Who is he?

What is he like?

What is he holding?

What is he saying?

What will happen next?

Different narrators

Write a description of the scene with the pirate as narrator.

....

....

....

....

....

....

....

What can they see?

What are they doing?

What can they hear?

Is anyone speaking?

How are they feeling?

What is going to happen?

Now, write your description with the person hiding as narrator.

....

....

....

....

....

....

....

....

Pirate treasure plan

Plan your story by making notes or drawing your ideas.

Characters

Setting

Beginning

Dilemma

Solution

Ending

Unit 3 – Ghost rider

Learning objectives

- To consider the different writing styles of classic poets.
- To experiment with active verbs and personification (Term 1, T10).
- To produce revised poems for reading aloud individually (Term 1, T10).

Ideas for using the activity sheets

Page 16: Ghost rider

- Look at examples of classic poems about related subjects (ghosts, the night, scary situations). Make a collection of words or phrases that are no longer used and decide on a modern-day translation for them. The children could use the list when completing the sheet and develop it into their own classic poem.
- Discuss positive and negative situations and how the type of language used can create a certain atmosphere. Make a class list of words that could be used to describe the scene earlier on when everything in the bedroom was calm and happy. The children could then work in pairs to make a list of words to portray the scene as pictured. Compare the finished lists. The children could use the lists to write a poem, starting from when the person went to bed.
- Ask the children to work In pairs to write a poem to develop fear and suspense, by describing the sounds the person hears in the dark. Consider using sound effects. They could perform the finished pieces in a darkened room and discuss which were the most effective and why.

Page 17: Ghostly personification

- Look at examples of personification in poetry. Discuss why it is used so much in poetry. Make a collection of active verbs to use. Ask the children to work in pairs to come up with a minimum of three different ideas for each line. Tell them to choose the best idea for a finished piece. Share their ideas.
- As a whole class, choose one of the line starters and compose a poem where each line starts with the same word(s); for example, The wind... The wind... Use personification for each line. The children could then work individually, using a different line.
- Organise the children into small groups and give each group one line to focus on. They should think of as many lines as possible, using personification. Share their best ideas to compose a class poem.

Page 18: Ghostly verses

- Revise the differences between personification, similes and metaphors. Look at examples in poems and discuss their impact. As a whole class, work on composing the first line of the poem in the three different ways. In pairs, the children could continue doing this and, when finished, use the ideas to compose a poem using their best lines.
- The children could use the completed sheet to experiment with the order of lines. They could work in pairs, cutting up both their sheets, re-arranging the ideas and using a combination of the two. Ask them to read out their finished poems.
- Look at a classic poem relevant to the theme. Discuss the structure used, language, mood created and so on. Work with the class to compose a poem in the style of that poet. Discuss how successful they have been. Are some of the verses more similar to the poet's style than others?

Ghost rider

Make notes around the picture.

What is outside?

How is the person in bed feeling?

What are they doing?

What is the book about?

When is it?

Where is it?

What sounds are there?

What can you see?

Make a collection of words to describe the scene.

Ghostly personification

Make a list of active verbs to use.

Think about the atmosphere/feeling that you wish to portray in your poem.
Complete the lines using personification.

Night time ....

The wind ....

Darkness ....

The door ....

Fear ....

My bed ....

Sleep ....

Edit your lines - changing word order, adding more description etc.

Ghostly verses

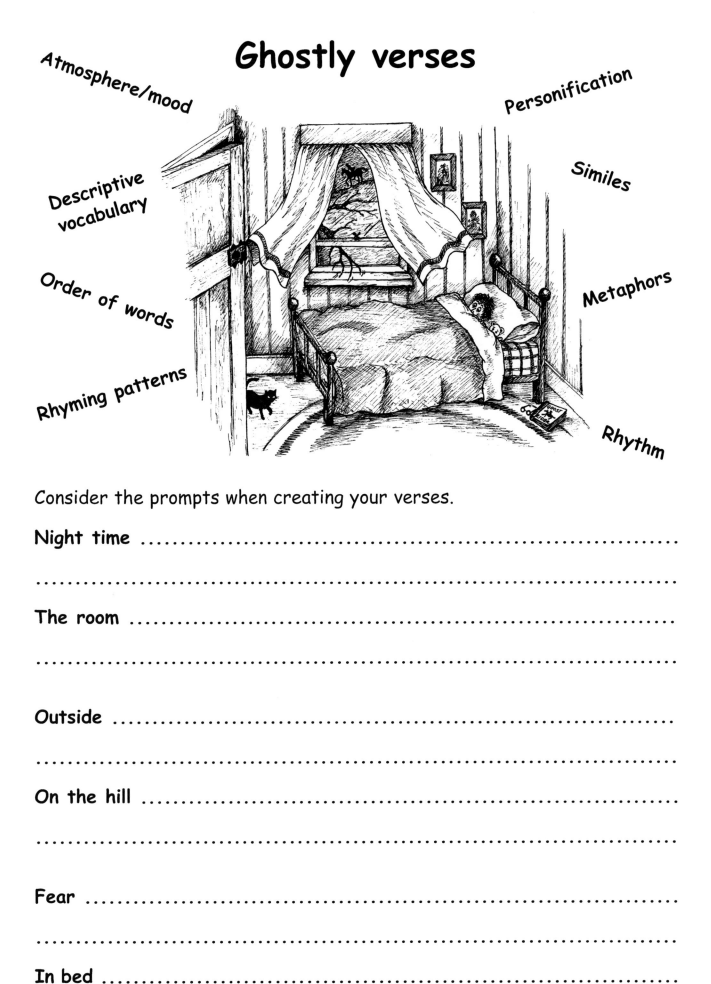

Atmosphere/mood

Personification

Descriptive vocabulary

Similes

Order of words

Metaphors

Rhyming patterns

Rhythm

Consider the prompts when creating your verses.

Night time ....

....

The room ....

....

Outside ....

....

On the hill ....

....

Fear ....

....

In bed ....

....

Unit 4 – Star couple

Learning objectives

- To develop a journalistic style (Term 1, T15).
- To use styles/conventions of journalism to report on imagined events (Term 1, T16).

Ideas for using the activity sheets

Page 21: Star Couple

- Look at a variety of magazine articles and newspaper reports. Discuss the language/style of writing used – does it vary depending on the publication? Who is the target audience? Tell the children which type of publication their report is for and ask them to complete the sheet, taking that into consideration.
- Discuss the difference between fact and opinion. Ask the children to think of examples for a familiar famous person. Look at an example of journalistic writing where there is a balance of fact and opinions. Discuss types of opinions that would not be appropriate/allowed; for example, that the person is lazy or mean. Are there any facts that would be inappropriate?
- Answer the questions as a whole class, to give a common set of facts. Discuss who is likely to give quotes about the stars. Make a list of people. The children could work in pairs, writing quotes that they think would be appropriate to the story. Then they could use the sheet to write a report, including the best of their quotes.

Page 22: Star headlines

- Make a class collection of headlines for display. Investigate different methods used, for example, alliteration, play on words. The children could work on computers, devising suitable headlines for the story. Encourage them to experiment with size and style of font.
- Look at headlines used in different publications. Discuss tabloid newspapers and the type of headline used. Ask the children to write headlines suitable for a tabloid paper.
- In small groups, the children could work on developing headlines that focus on one style of writing; for example, rhyming words. Share the most successful ones with the class.
- Make a collection of headlines that use the names of the important people in the report. Give the star couple names. Challenge the children to make up headlines using their names.

Page 23: Star Couple report

- Look at examples of headlines and report summaries. What do they do? Why are they important? Discuss how they draw the reader into the report and encourage them to read more. Complete the summary for the report as a whole class. The children could then work individually to complete the piece.
- Working in pairs, one child could take on the role of reporter and the other the role of one of the stars pictured. The reporter asks suitable questions and records responses. They could use the notes to write a shared report.
- Ask the children to provide an alternative picture for the report. This could be drawn or taken from a newspaper/magazine, and be of a chosen celebrity. They could work individually, planning a story and then writing the report. The class could make their own newspaper or magazine.

Star couple

Make notes around the picture.

When is it?

Who are they?

Where is it?

What is happening?

Why are they there?

What are they famous for?

Write down some more details to use in your journalistic report.
Write down facts and opinions that you think your readers will be interested in.

Facts	Opinions
....	....
....	....
....	....
....	....
....	....
....	....

Write down quotes from eyewitnesses.

....

....

....

Star headlines

Make up some catchy headlines for the story.

Short and snappy.

Play on words.

Big, bold letters.

Make it eye-catching.

Make it funny.

Rhyming words.

Use alliteration.

Make a list of words you could use for a headline about this picture.

[   ]

Reported by: (catchy headline)

(summary of the story)

....

....

....

....

....

....

[   ]   (caption)

(main events - include facts, opinions and quotes)

....

....

....

....

....

....

....

....

....

....

(ending - current status, future plans)

....

....

....

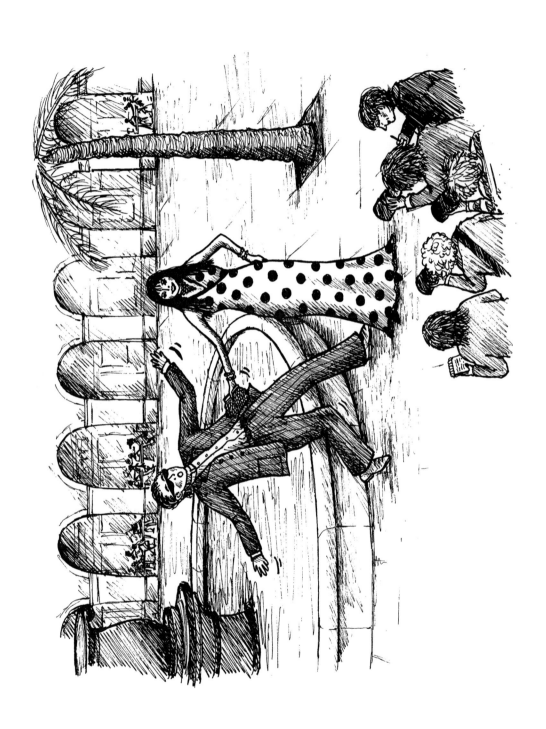

Unit 5 – Famous four

Learning objectives

- To develop skills in biographical/autobiographical writing (Term 1, T14).
- To compose a biographical account (Term 1, T14).
- To organise writing in paragraphs.

Ideas for using the activity sheets

Page 26: Famous four

- Prior to the lesson, ask the children to make a list of people who have had biographies written about them (perhaps as homework). Make a class list and categorise them according to the reasons for their fame. Look at the characters on the sheet and decide what their main achievement could be. Challenge the children to choose a less obvious achievement for the chosen character.
- Look at examples of biographies. List the basic information included in each one. Discuss the sequence of information. The children could work in pairs to complete the sheet, considering the character they have chosen.
- The children could use the completed sheet to write a CV for the character. Look at examples of layout for a CV and discuss which aspects of the sheet would be included. Are more details/facts required in parts? Ask the children to swap completed sheets, and in small groups, decide what alternative career the character could have, giving reasons.

Page 27: Famous for what?

- Look at an example of a biography and highlight the paragraphs in the text. Discuss what each tells us and why these facts have been separated. Ask the children to complete the sheet, for their chosen character. Share the finished work. The children could read out a paragraph and the class has to guess which paragraph they have read out (1,2,3,4 or 5).
- Choose a character to work on as a class. Scribe the children's ideas. Focus on making strong opening and closing paragraphs.
- Look at how verbs are used. Read an extract from a biography and discuss the tense used and the role of passive verbs. Go through examples of passive and active verbs so that they are confident in identifying them.
- In pairs, the children could research the life of a real famous person. They could use books or the internet to find facts and information for each paragraph.

Page 28: You're famous!

- The children could work in pairs, interviewing each other as if they were a famous person. They could record each other's ideas on the sheet.
- Compare how a biography and an autobiography are written. Make a list of differences and highlight the key areas for writing an autobiography. Ask the children to use their completed sheet to write their own autobiography.
- Ask the children to use their completed sheet to prepare a talk they might give as a visiting celebrity to the school. Discuss what type of character would interest the children and how they could interest/inspire the audience. They could deliver their completed speeches to small groups or the class.

Famous four

1. Choose ONE of the characters.

2. Cut him/her out and stick the picture in the frame.

3. Make notes around the frame.

When was he/she born?

What were his/her parents' jobs?

Where did he/she grow up?

What was he/she like at school?

What was his/her childhood like?

What did he/she do after he/she left school?

What did he/she want to be when he/she was young?

At what age did he/she become famous?

Name:

What is he/she famous for?

Is he/she still alive?

What are his/her special achievements?

Famous for what?

Write a biography for ONE of the characters shown.
Use the prompts to help organise each paragraph.

_____ (person's name)

Paragraph 1
(opening - introduce person, what he/she is famous for, main achievement)

....

....

Paragraph 2
(when/where born, family details)

....

....

Paragraph 3
(school days, childhood, dreams for future career)

....

....

....

Paragraph 4
(development of career, problems encountered, family, wealth)

....

....

....

Paragraph 5
(ending - reinforce reasons for fame, future plans)

....

....

....

You're famous!

Imagine that you are famous! Draw a picture of yourself.
Then, make notes to help you write your biography.

What did you do when you left school?

When did you first discover your talent?

What are you famous for?

What are your special achievements?

What do you want to do in the future?

Where did you grow up?

What did your parents do?

Have you any childhood memories?

What were you like at school?

What did you want to be when you grew up?

When were you born?

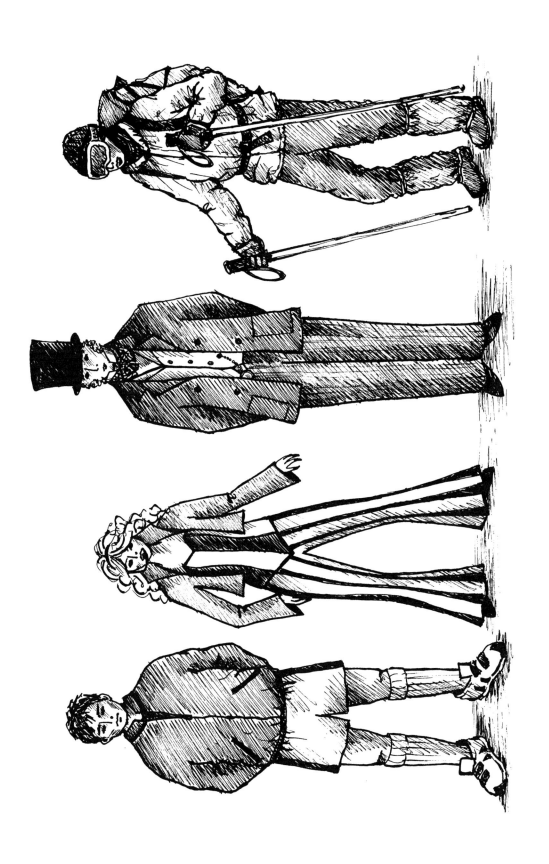

Unit 6 – Searching

Learning objectives

- To write a story using flashbacks (Term 2, T11).
- To write alternative endings, using genre models (Term 2, T10).
- To study in depth one genre, producing an extended piece (Term 2, T12).

Ideas for using the activity sheets

Page 31: Searching

- Look at extracts from mystery stories by different authors. The children could work in pairs, writing down the common themes, settings, characters and so on. Devise a class recipe to make a mystery story. The children could use their completed sheet to write this part of the story using the recipe.
- Look at characters in mystery stories. As a class, write character profiles for the two children. Decide what other characters would be needed in the story. The children could work on drawing and developing the profiles for these new characters. Share their ideas.
- Discuss the setting on the sheet and decide, as a class, what the atmosphere would be like. How can they create that feeling? Discuss the use of description, sentence length, dialogue and so on. Ask the children to write a description of the scene, with the emphasis on creating a tense atmosphere.

Page 32: Searching flashback

- Look at examples of flashbacks in mysteries. Discuss how this scene could involve a character thinking back to an earlier time to solve the mystery. Make a list of what could have happened earlier that day. Which ideas would help them to find a solution? Ask the children to choose one option and develop this as a flashback.
- As a class, make a basic plan for the story and decide on each character's role. Introduce a detective who has come to solve the mystery. Ask for volunteers to each take on the role of a character and answer the detective's questions. Discuss how each character's version of events could be used as a flashback in the story.
- Focus on the briefcase as an important part of the mystery. Ask the children to work in pairs to make a list of all the items that could be in the case. Tell them to make notes as to how each item could be a clue to, or evidence for, something else. They then choose their best idea and use this when writing the flashback.

Page 33: Search ending

- Carry out research into how a particular author ends their mystery stories. Can the class see similarities across different stories? Discuss the style of the author. The children could plan different endings in the style of the author studied.
- Is the briefcase a red herring? Discuss what this means, and decide what real clues there could be in the room they are searching. Challenge different groups of children to develop alternative endings, using a specific item or place in the room pictured.
- Decide who could be hiding behind the curtain and how important they are to the story. Make a list of possibilities for their character. The children could plan their endings from the viewpoint of the person who is hiding.

Searching

Make notes around the picture.

Where is it?

When is it?

What has happened before?

Who is in the car?

Who is behind the curtain?

What will happen next?

Who are they?

Why are they there?

How are they feeling?

What are they looking for?

Why?

What have they found?

Searching flashback

Write a plan of what happened
before this scene.

Imagine you are one of the two children.
Use your plan to write what happened earlier as a flashback.

We found what we were looking for! Everything made sense now.

Earlier that day, ...

....

....

....

....

....

....

....

....

Search ending

How does the mystery end? Plan three different endings.

Do they take something from the briefcase?

What is it?

Are they caught?

Do they use the computer?

Do they leave the room?

Do they help someone?

Unit 7 – Space landing

Learning objectives

- To use different genres to write short extracts (Term 2, T10).
- To write a story using flashbacks/story within a story (Term 2, T11).
- To study in depth one genre, producing an extended piece (Term 2, T12).

Ideas for using the activity sheets

Page 36: Space landing

- Research science fiction stories and films. Discuss the similarities/differences between various aspects such as plot, characters and setting. Choose one of these aspects and ask the children to write a comparison between their ideas for the sheet and other stories of the same genre. Make a display of their work and research materials.
- Complete the sheet as a class. Make a story plan and discuss how the ideas would be organised in a book (chapters). The children could work in pairs, creating a contents page and giving each chapter a title. Share their finished work. They could read out a chapter title while the class works out which part of the story it relates to.
- Use the sheet to plan a story for a piece of extended writing to be completed over a series of lessons. At the start of each lesson, focus on one particular aspect of writing; for example, story beginnings, writing in paragraphs, use of flashbacks. The children could support each other in revising their writing. This work would be ideally created on computer to allow for constant revision and editing. The completed pieces could make a class anthology.

Page 37: Space landing extract

- Use role play to allow the children to 'experience' the scene first hand. Hot seat volunteers as the two main characters, to find out how they are feeling and what they might say to each other in this situation. The children could then use the experience to help them complete the sheet.
- Look at examples of flashbacks in stories. Discuss how this scene could involve a character thinking back to an earlier time. What triggered that thought? Make a list of their ideas. Ask the children to write their extract with a flashback included.
- Look at extracts of dialogue where the author varies the way the dialogue is presented. Is it always necessary to say who is talking? Revise the layout and punctuation of dialogue. Make a class list of synonyms of the word 'said'. The children could work in pairs, each deciding what one of the characters would say. Ask them to write the extract with dialogue.

Page 38: Space aliens

- Look at examples of aliens portrayed in stories/films. Discuss which of the aliens is the children's favourite and why. Write a profile of the alien on the board, listing aspects that they will need to consider when creating their own alien (appearance, character, language and so on). Ask the children to use the list to help them develop their own alien.
- Look at examples of a story within a story. Discuss how the aliens could offer another story to run alongside the spaceship landing. How would it be separated within the story? The children could use the sheet alongside the 'Space landing' sheet, developing a piece of writing that includes a story within a story.
- Ask the children to write a story from the viewpoint of the planet's inhabitants. Describe what they saw when the spaceship landed and how it affected them. What did they think

Space landing

Make notes around the picture.

Where are they?

When is it?

How did they get there?

Describe the setting.

What will happen next?

Who/what is watching?

Who is in the ship?

What are they doing? Why?

How do they feel?

Describe the space ship.

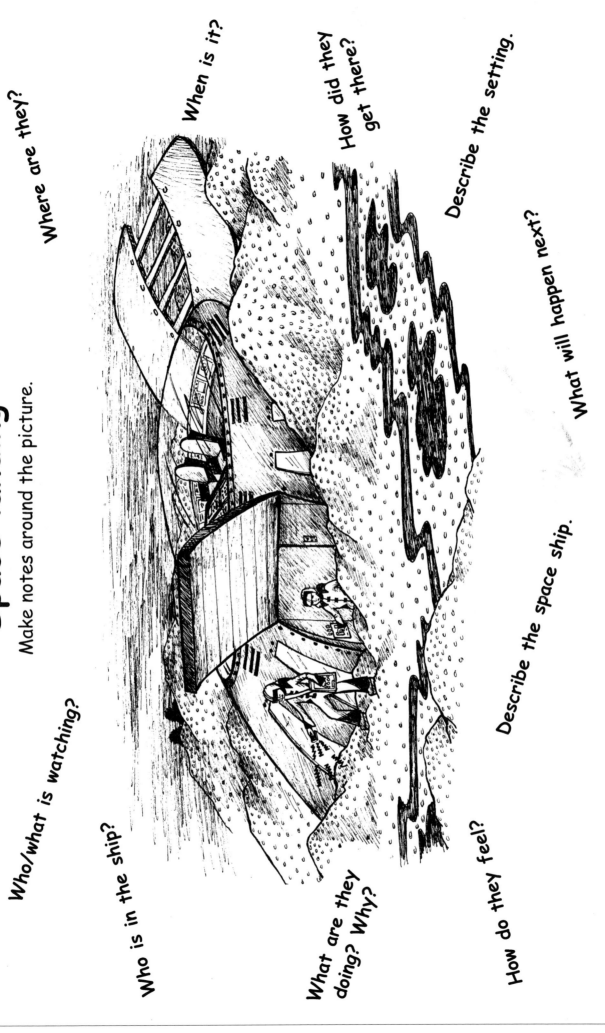

Space landing extract

What would each character say?

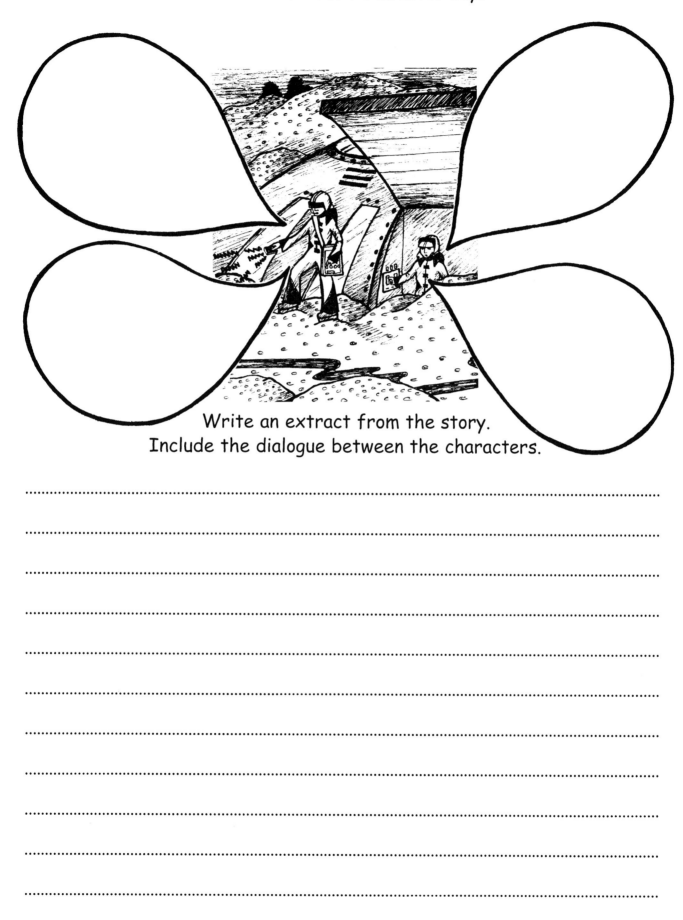

Write an extract from the story.
Include the dialogue between the characters.

....
....
....
....
....
....
....
....
....
....

Space aliens

What is the story behind the inhabitants of the planet?
Draw a picture of them and make notes.

What is the problem?

What are they going to do?

What do they think of the visitors?

What effect will the visitors have?

Do they travel to other planets?

Is there a large population?

Where do they live on the planet?

Do they speak a different language?

What do they eat?

Do they live in groups/families?

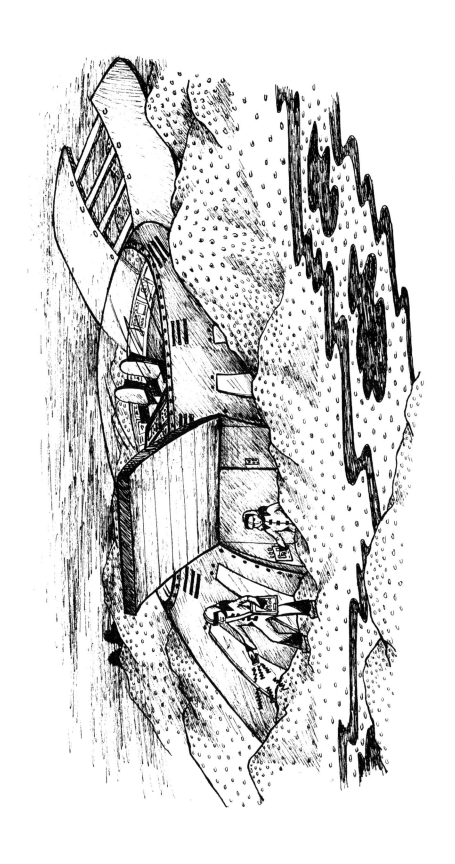

Unit 8 – Dreaming

Learning objectives

- To write poems in a range of forms (Term 2, T10).
- To convey moods and feelings in poetic writing.
- To plan, revise and redraft poems (Term 2, T12).

Ideas for using the activity sheets

Page 41: Dreaming

- Look at poetry that has a set pattern of lines/syllables such as kenning, tanka, haiku or cinquain. The children could use their completed sheet to develop poems of different forms. Share their most successful poems. Which type was hardest to compose? Redraft and present the poems as a class book.
- Use completed sheets to develop ideas for performance poems based on models. Look at existing poems – can they use their ideas in the same style as someone else's poem? They could work in pairs, drafting and redrafting their ideas. They need to practise performing their verses. Have they been able to use the poet's style in their composition?
- Look at rhyming patterns in poetry. Ask the children to complete the sheet in pairs, trying to find words that rhyme. They could then use the completed sheet to write sets of rhyming couplets. Bring their ideas together and compose a poem as a whole class.

Page 42: Dream diary

- Revise the use of metaphors, similes and personification in poetry. Discuss which the children feel will be most successful for this subject matter. Organise them into small groups and ask them to compose examples of each, for a group poem. They could write each line on a separate piece of paper and try out different orders to develop their final piece. Perform them to the class.
- Discuss how dreams make us feel, and what kinds of emotions each of the scenarios pictured would evoke. Can these emotions develop and change through the dream? For example, with the football match – tension, nerves, leading to the joy of winning. Ask the children to choose one scenario and compose their diary page, with an emphasis on portraying the feelings/mood of their character as the dream develops.
- Look at the use of assonance in poetry. Act as scribe, developing a class poem on one dream scenario. Ask the children to give their ideas for the inclusion of assonance. They could then work on their own diary page.

Page 43: My Dream

- Discuss how dreams differ from nightmares. What feelings do you have during and after a nightmare? List their ideas. Ask the children to complete the sheet with an idea that starts as a dream and ends as a nightmare. Develop it into a poem, going through the different stages.
- The children could use the completed sheet to write a narrative poem starting with going to bed, working through a dream sequence and ending with being woken up the next morning.
- What dream would a famous pop star or football player have? Ask the children to complete the sheet as if they were a celebrity. Share their finished poems – can the others guess who the famous person is?

Dreaming

Label the dreams and make notes about each one.
Use the prompts to help.

What has happened?

Where is it?

What does he do?

How does it end?

What is the dream?

How does he feel?

What can he hear?

What can he see?

Dream diary

Imagine that you are the boy.
Write a poem about your dream, as a diary page.

Similes

Metaphors

Rhythm

Personification

Rhyming patterns

Vocabulary

Assonance

Moods/feelings

Dear diary,

Last night ....

....

....

....

....

....

....

....

....

....

My dream

What is your dream? Draw it in the bubble.

What can you see?

What can you hear?

Where is it?

When is it?

How does it end?

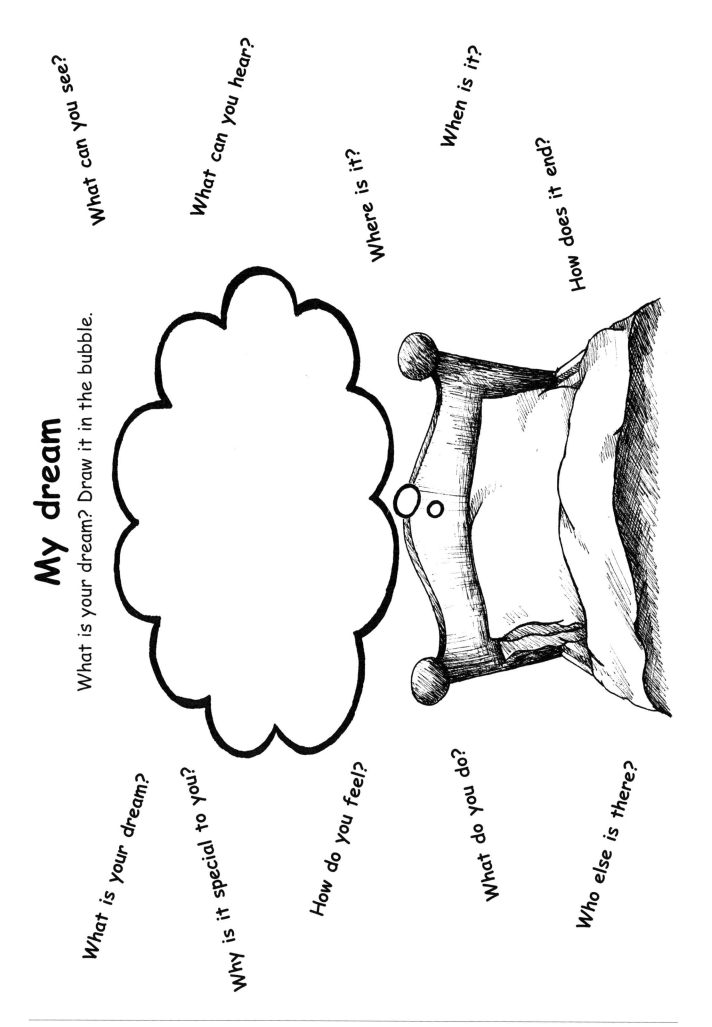

What is your dream?

Why is it special to you?

How do you feel?

What do you do?

Who else is there?

Unit 9 – The trench

Learning objectives

- To write story, using flashbacks/story within a story (Term 2, T11).
- To convey the passing of time (Term 2, T11).
- To write extracts from a story in a historical setting (Term 2, T10).

Ideas for using the activity sheets

Page 46: The trench

- Use the internet and resource books to research life in the trenches. Collect details to give the class a feel for what life was like. Ask the children to use ideas from their completed sheet to write a diary entry for one of the soldiers. The class could write a series of entries that describe certain situations and events.
- Look at methods used by authors to convey the passing of time. Look at the picture and discuss which methods could be used. Would time be passing slowly at this point? When would it seem to speed up? Ask the children to write an extract with one of the soldiers as narrator. Tell them to start when there is nothing happening and develop the story into a battle scene. Tell them to use the methods discussed that show the passage of time.
- Ask the children to use the completed sheet to develop a play scene. They could work in pairs, deciding on their lines and how the characters would deliver them in the situation that they are in. They could perform their scene to the class.

Page 47: Memories of home

- Discuss times when the children might have been away from home. What things did they miss? Discuss how this made them feel at the time. Make a list of words to describe their feelings when homesick, and those they could use when describing their happy memories. The children could use the lists to help them write the flashback.
- Ask the children to write the letter that the soldier is reading. Who is it from? Are they related? What are they doing? Remind them to include some reference to something that would trigger his thoughts of happier times.
- Discuss what else could remind him of happier times. Make a class list of objects, sounds, smells and phrases that could take the place of the letter. The children could work in pairs, writing the dialogue between the two soldiers, introducing the trigger and memory into the conversation. Does it mean something to both soldiers?

Page 48: Letter from the trench

- Act as a scribe, writing a letter to his friend who has returned home injured. Include how he really feels and the worries he has about the war. The children could use this as a model for writing a letter home to his mother. Discuss which details he would include from the first letter and how he would take care not to worry her.
- The children could swap their completed letters and write a reply to the soldier. They need to respond to what he has written and give him information about things that they are doing.
- Look at the use of letters in books. Discuss how the letters could be used to move from one setting to the other (home to trench). Could each chapter start with a letter? Give the children a chapter title or point in the story to use to write the letter.

The trench

Make notes around the picture.

When is it?

Where are they?

Who are they?

Describe the setting.

What are they doing?

What can they hear?

How do they feel?
Why?

What can they see?

Who else is there with them?

Who is the letter from?

Memories of home

The letter has made the soldier think of home.

Make a list of possible memories.
↓

Now choose one incident and write it as a flashback, with the soldier as narrator.

I read the letter. It reminded me of ....

....

....

....

....

....

....

....

....

Letter from the trench

What has happened?

How does he feel?

What are conditions like?

What is he missing?

What is he hoping for?

Write his reply to the letter.
Use the prompts to help.

....

....

....

....

....

....

....

....

....

....

....

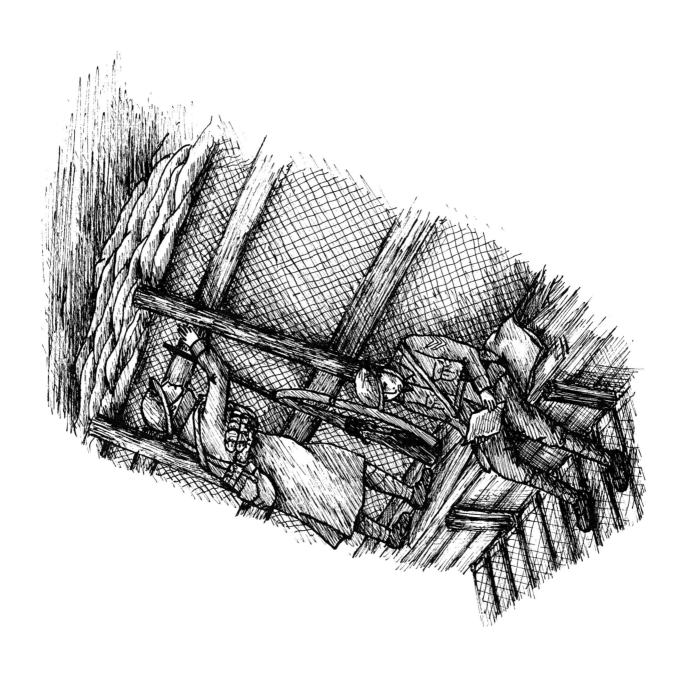

Unit 10 – Building site

Learning objectives

- To construct effective arguments (Term 3, T18).
- To write a balanced report of a controversial issue (Term 3, T19).
- To understand the features of formal language (Term 3, T17).

Ideas for using the activity sheets

Page 51: Building site

- Look at local papers to find out about any controversial developments in the area. Discuss why there are problems. Make a list of developments that generally cause controversy and the reasons why. Ask the children to complete the sheet in pairs, imagining that it is a local issue.
- The children could use their completed sheet to write a newspaper report about the development. They will need to decide what it will be when built, and the preferences of the people voicing their objections. Are they planning to take any action? Reinforce the need for their report to be balanced. Can they think of a good headline?
- The children could complete the sheet and decide which viewpoint they support. Group them with others of the same view and ask them to write a list of all the reasons supporting their choice. Share these with the class – which is their strongest reason?

Page 52: Balanced report

- Look at how evidence can be used to support certain viewpoints. Complete the sheet, looking at one choice, with the class. In small groups, the children could discuss where they think they could get the evidence to support reasons for and against the development. They could make lists for and against. Discuss their ideas with the whole class.
- Use the completed sheet to write a balanced report. Discuss how the information should be organised. What would be in the introductory paragraph? How would they arrange the main points? What would need to be in the conclusion? Display a basic plan to support the children's writing.
- Ask the children to look at examples of reports to analyse the formal language. Collect typical words and expressions to make a class bank of ideas. Discuss the use of the impersonal voice, imperative verbs, formal language and so on. Ask the children to use all their research and their ideas noted on the sheet to write a balanced report.

Page 53: Building site argument

- The children could use ideas from the sheet to design a poster or leaflet to support their argument. Discuss which information is important, and the need to make it eye-catching. Display their finished work and discuss which are the most effective posters and why.
- Use completed sheets in a debate on the development. Agree rules for the debate. The children could work in small groups, amalgamating their ideas, making banners, organising a spokesperson and so on. A group could also play the role of the developer.
- Ask the children to use their completed sheet to write their argument. Discuss the layout and the need for formal language. Ask them to read their finished argument to someone at home and record their comments about the effectiveness of it. Were there particular points or words that persuaded them? Feed their comments back to the class.

Building site

Decide what each person would like the new development to be.
Give reasons to support their choice.

Balanced report

Choose a person from the picture. Make notes about him/her.

Age:

Gender:

Occupation:

Interests:

Idea for development:

Now, write down all the reasons supporting his/her choice.
Balance this with reasons against it.

For......................

....

....

....

....

....

....

....

....

....

Against......................

....

....

....

....

....

....

....

....

....

Building site argument

Decide what development you would like to see on the site.
Draw and label your idea.

List reasons to support your idea.
Put them in order, starting with your strongest argument.

....

....

....

....

....

....

....

Make a collection of words and phrases you could use to help persuade
others to support your argument.

WRITING SPRINGBOARDS

Unit 11 – Book blurb

Learning objectives

- To write a brief synopsis of a text (Term 3, T10).
- To write summaries of books, deciding on priorities (Term 3, T9).
- To write a brief helpful review tailored to a real audience (Term 3, T11).

Ideas for using the activity sheets

Page 56: Book blurb

- Look at book front covers and discuss how they give clues to the genre. What sorts of images are used? Make a class display of cover designs grouped according to type/theme. Decide on the possible genre for the book on the sheet. The children could complete the sheet, taking this into account.
- As a class, consider the work of a particular author. Imagining that the same author has written this book, the children could complete the sheet using answers that would be typical for that author's style.
- Ask the children to use the information from the completed sheet to write a review of the book. This could be for use in a children's magazine or take the form of a television review. With the latter, the children could work in small groups, developing a short talk on the book, for television.

Page 57: Blurb layout

- Ask the children to look at a collection of different books to find out what is included on the back cover and how it is set out. Discuss similarities in style and format. They could complete the sheet considering their researched information.
- Decide, as a class, on a basic plan for the story. Discuss what sort of detail is included in the blurb and how it is written. Act as a scribe, modelling how to set out and write the information.
- Look at the use of quotes/recommendations. What effect do they have on the reader? Do the children look for books written for their age group? How is this shown? As a class, work on a synopsis of the story. Then, ask the children to work in pairs to write quotes and recommendations that could be included. Share their ideas with the class.

Page 58: Cover design

- The children could redesign the front and back cover for a book that they are familiar with. Discuss what they must include in the illustration (particular characters, clues to genre) and in the information on the back. Ask another class to evaluate the new designs in comparison with the original.
- Give the children a specific genre to design for, such as horror and humorous. The children could work in pairs, initially on rough ideas and then on the finished piece. Make a class display.
- Ask the children to plan a book that is the next in a series by a popular children's author. They need to research characters, typical settings, story lines that would be suitable for the author's next book.
- Look at cover designs for non-fiction books. How do they differ from fiction books? The children could design their own cover for a non-fiction book on the topic of their choice.

Book blurb

Make notes around the picture.

What age is it aimed at?

What is the genre?

Who are the main characters?

What is the plot?

Can you think of a good title?

Where is it set?

When is it?

Who is the author?

Have they written other books?

What is special about this book?

Blurb layout

Target age

Reviews

Quotes

Questions

Genre

Synopsis of book

Characters

Short extract

Write the blurb for this book. Use the prompts to help.

ISBN 123456
9 876 54321

U.K. £6.99

Cover design

Draw the front cover and write the blurb for a book.
Use the prompts to help.

Title Genre Synopsis of book Characters Illustrator Author

Quotes Questions Short extract Reviews Target age Publisher

ISBN 123456
9 876 54321
U.K. £6.99

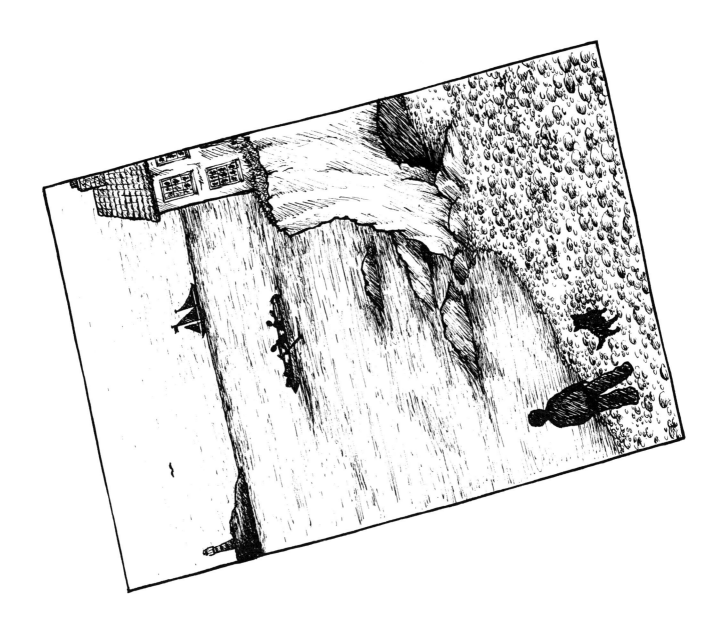

Unit 12 – Holding on

Learning objectives

- To lengthen and shorten sentences to change pace and mood.
- To use setting to create and reflect changes in mood.
- To write an extended story, worked on over time (Term 3, T14).

Ideas for using the activity sheets

Page 61: Holding on

- Look at paragraph examples from adventure stories. Discuss the language used to create excitement and tension. How is sentence length used to make a scene more dramatic? As a whole class, complete the sheet on an OHT, trying to use powerful verbs and adjectives that reflect the mood. Ask the children to use the sheet to write a paragraph that really captures the atmosphere.
- Make a class list of words/phrases they could use to describe how they would feel if they were in this situation. Ask the children to write an account of the scene as if they were one of the main characters. They should include a description of their feelings and thoughts about the situation.
- Explore different ways to write the opening of this scene. List the children's ideas on the board. Which ones create a dramatic effect? Ask the children to use these ideas and, working in pairs, create the scene for a radio drama. They could record it and play it back to the class.

Page 62: Holding on – the mood

- Look at extracts from stories where sentence length has been used to add pace. Act as a scribe, writing a description of the scene. The children could work in pairs, experimenting with shortening sentences within the text. Share their finished pieces – how successful have they been in making it more dramatic?
- Discuss the setting for the scene. How would it have seemed before the girl fell? As a class, make a list of positive vocabulary to describe the setting. Then make a list of words to describe the current situation (negative vocabulary). The children could write a description of the scene before the incident and follow through to the scene pictured. Emphasise the need to change the vocabulary to affect the mood.
- Use dialogue between the characters to create tension. How can they portray panic and fear by what they are saying? Look at the use of ellipsis to convey a character's thoughts. The children could work in pairs, role playing the conversation and then use their ideas to write the scene.

Page 63: Holding on – story plan

- Use the plan over a series of lessons to write an extended story. Each lesson, focus on one aspect that is appropriate to that stage of the story. The children could edit and improve their work before producing a completed story. They could share stories with another class and ask for responses (perhaps devising a review sheet for completion).
- They could use the story plan to design a front cover and write the blurb for the book. Make a class display.
- Complete the plan as a class and then divide the story between small groups. Each group then works on writing that part. Bring all the parts together and edit as a class.

Holding on

Make notes around the picture.

When is it?

Where is it?

Describe the setting.

What is the weather like?

How will the problem be resolved?

Who are they?

Why were they there?

What has happened?

How are they feeling?

Is there anyone else there?

Holding on – the mood

Make a collection of words to describe the situation.
Do they portray the negative mood?

Now use them to write a description of the scene.
Experiment with short sentences to create a dramatic mood.

What are they saying?

Holding on - story plan

Plan out the key events in your story.

Where did it start?

What were they doing on the cliff top?

Why were they there?

How did she fall over the edge?

How is she saved?

Who helps them?

How does it end?

Unit 13 – Fun fair

Learning objectives

- To write a sequence of poems linked by theme or form (Term 3, T13).
- To use different styles/structures in the poem.
- To revise, redraft and present a poem.

Ideas for using the activity sheets

Page 66: Fun fair

- Read various poems about fun fairs. Discuss their similarities and make a collection of words and phrases used. Look at the structure of one poem and identify the rhyming pattern. Scribe a verse for the poem as a whole class, using this structure. The children could work in pairs to continue the poem.
- Write a very basic poem before the lesson. The children could complete the sheet and use their ideas to work on improving the basic poem by changing word order, adding interesting vocabulary, making it rhyme and so on.
- Look at rhyming patterns in poetry. Ask the children to complete the sheet in pairs, trying to find words that rhyme. They can then use the completed sheet to write sets of rhyming couplets. Bring their ideas together and compose a poem as a whole class.
- Use the ideas to write a narrative poem. Scribe the start and ask the children to complete it.

Page 67: Fun fair haikus/tankas

- Look, in depth, at examples of both forms. Discuss what sort of feelings they evoke. Ask the children to work in pairs to develop their own ideas using their bank of words related to the theme.
- Look at poems about fairgrounds. Make a collection of words and phrases from them. Ask the children to use the ideas to write haikus and tankas.
- Split the children into groups and ask them to write as many lines as they can with a given number of syllables. Tell them to bring their ideas together with another group to compose haiku and tanka poems. They can change lines and discuss the best order, so that the final poems are the best order and choice of line.

Page 68: My fun fair

- Challenge small groups to make a verse that rhymes. They need to consider which rhyming pattern they wish to adopt and try out different ideas in draft form, then make a final draft that they all agree is the best. Ask them to read them out to the class and discuss the most successful parts and identify the rhyming pattern. Bring all their ideas together to make a class poem on the fair.
- The children could work in pairs to develop the ideas into a performance poem. Tell them to make up a chorus, including actions and sound effects. They could perform them to the class.
- Look at different descriptive styles used in poetry such as similes, metaphors and personification. Could they be used in their verse? Ask the children to compose a verse trying to use the styles discussed. They could work in pairs to revise and redraft their verses.
- Ask the children to make up an imaginary ride. Discuss how it could be magical. They could write a poem about their experience on the ride. Tell them to include a description of their emotions during the experience.

Fun fair

Make notes around the picture.

Feelings

Shapes

People

Rides

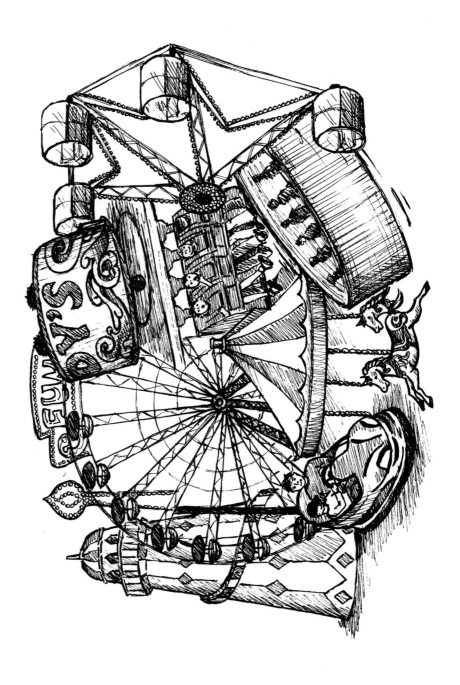

Smells   Colours

Movements

Sounds

Fun fair haikus/tankas

Make a collection of descriptive words and phrases you could use.

↓

Haiku
(3 lines of 5, 7, 5 syllables)
Write haikus about the fair.

....

....

....

....

....

....

....

....

....

Tanka
(5 lines of 5, 7, 5, 7, 7 syllables)
Write tankas about the fair.

....

....

....

....

....

....

....

....

....

....

My fun fair

Draw your favourite part of a fun fair. Write a verse about it.

<u>Helpful hints</u>
1. Decide what style your verse will be.
2. Write down your ideas.
3. Improve the lines by adding or taking out words.
4. Change the order of the lines, if needed.
5. Read aloud and check that you are happy with it!

....

....

....

....

....

....

....

....

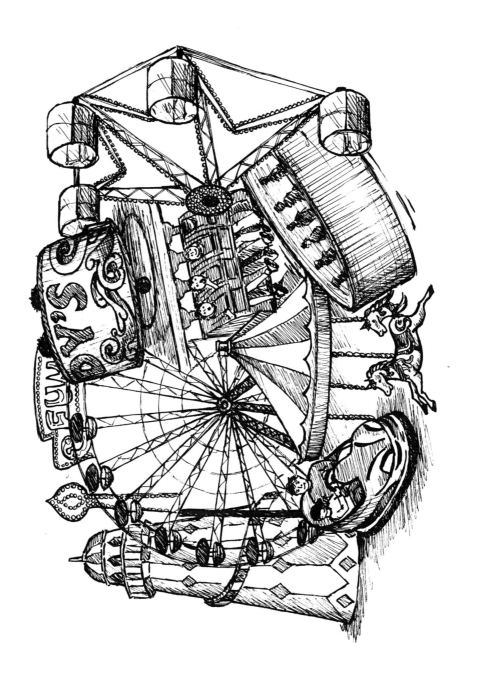

Unit 14 – The chief

Learning objectives

- To develop character descriptions.
- To elicit a response to characters through what is written.
- To change the nature/profile of a character.

Ideas for using the activity sheets

Page 71: The chief

- Ask the children to find out about the history/lifestyles of Native Americans. Discuss what role the character could have and how he could be portrayed. Ask the children to work in small groups to hot seat someone in the role of the chief. They could record their answers and ideas on the sheet.
- Discuss how this character could be seen as both wise and powerful. Make a list of words and phrases that suggest someone who is wise and powerful. The children could use these words to complete the sheet, and follow this up by writing a poem about him. Discuss how the poems make the reader react to the character.
- Look at biographies about characters in history. Decide, as a class, what special things the chief could have been remembered for. Make a character profile of him. The children could use this information to write his biography.

Page 72: The chief's character

- Discuss how we know whether a character is good or bad. Is it always stated in a text? Ask the children to role play a meeting with the chief where he would be a bad person. Discuss afterwards and record the phrases/words that they used to describe his bad qualities. Then role play with him as a good character and again record the responses.
- Provide the class with a basic description of the meeting. Discuss how this doesn't give an insight into the character. Ask the children to work in pairs, improving the description and suggesting what sort of character he is through their writing. Share their completed work.
- The children could write a letter to a friend, telling them about their meeting with the chief. They need to include details about the reason for the meeting – was it arranged or accidental? How did he make them feel? Why?

Page 73: The chief's diary

- Ask the children to decide what sort of person each characters is. They could make a list of qualities for each. Acting as a scribe, write the diary entry from the chief's point of view. The children could then work individually on writing a diary page for the other character, about the same meeting.
- Ask the children to write the meeting as a scene from a playscript. They could use stage directions to portray each character's qualities. Perform the scenes to the class and discuss their responses to the characters.
- Use the two characters to secure skills in writing dialogue. Discuss layout, punctuation and so on. Can they use adverbs to help describe reactions? Look at the use of ellipses to convey a character's thoughts.

The chief

Make notes around the picture.

What is his name?

Where does he live?

How old is he?

What does he do?

What is his position
in the tribe?

What family has he got?

What do others
think of him?

Describe what he
is wearing.

Describe his face.

How is he feeling? Why?

The chief's character

Is he a good or bad person?

How does he greet you?

What is your first impression?

Are there any movements?

What is he thinking?

What does he say?

What is his voice like?

How does he react to you?

How does he make you feel?

Does his facial expression change?

Imagine that you have a meeting with the chief.
Write down what happens, making sure that you give clues to his character through what you write.

....

....

....

....

....

....

....

....

....

The chief's diary

Draw another character. Imagine that they meet each other.

Does he like him/her?

Is there a problem?

How does he react?

What is he thinking?

Name?

Good or bad?

Do they know each other?

Why have they met?

Write an entry in the chief's diary, describing the meeting and how he feels about the other person.

(date) ....

....

....

....

....

....

....

....

....

....

....

Unit 15 – Sun safe

Learning objectives

- To write explanatory texts (Term 3, T22).
- To select appropriate style/form to suit specific purpose (Term 3, T22).
- To secure control of impersonal writing (Term 3, T20).

Ideas for using the activity sheets

Page 76: Sun safe

- Look at websites/leaflets/products that give advice on sun safety. Discuss the time of year when most advice is given and which format would reach the most people. Ask the children to use the collected information to help them complete the sheet.
- Prior to looking at the sheet, ask the children to list all the things they think they should do to keep safe in the sun. Share their ideas, looking at which aspects they are all familiar with. Look at the sheet together and add any relevant suggestions to the list. Discuss the need for explanations to give clear reasons in each case. The children could use the list and write explanations for the five most important rules.
- Ask the children to use the completed sheet to design and make a leaflet about sun safety.

Page 77: Sun safe fact sheet

- Look at an example of an explanatory text. Highlight the use of passive verbs. How would they be written as active verbs? Model writing part of the text using passive verbs. Review the writing – is the style correct? How would it sound if the verbs were active? Ask the children to complete the sheet, concentrating on verbs in the passive.
- Discuss the need for clear, concise sentences in an explanatory text. Ask the children to experiment with different ways of writing a given fact about the sun. Share their ideas with the class and discuss which are/are not appropriate to impersonal writing. Complete the introduction as a class to reinforce the need for clear information. They could then complete the sheet individually.
- Look at ways of setting out rules (use of bullet points, numbers). Work as a whole class, writing safety rules together. Then the children could use the rules to experiment, on the computer, with different layouts.

Page 78: Sun safe poster

- Look at examples of posters giving safety information. Discuss the layout and how the information is put across. Look at sentence length and use of illustrations to reinforce key points. Then ask the children to complete the poster.
- The children could design the poster for younger children. What do they have to consider? Discuss the need for simple words, lots of visual help and perhaps a character that would attract the younger audience.
- Enlarge the sheet to A3 and have children working in small groups. They could experiment with text size and font type (for impact) on the computer. They should discuss and experiment with the layout before sticking the printouts from the computer onto the poster. These could then be displayed around the school as safety posters.

Sun safe

Make a list of things you should and shouldn't do to keep safe in the sun.
Give reasons for each one. The picture will help.

....

....

....

....

....

....

....

....

....

....

Sun safe fact sheet

Write a fact sheet explaining how to keep safe in the sun.

<u>Introduction</u> (general information on the effects of the sun)

....

....

....

....

....

....

<u>How to keep safe</u> (list key safety rules with clear explanations)

....

....

....

....

....

....

....

....

....

....

<u>Conclusion</u> (make some closing statements reinforcing safety aspects)

....

....

....

....

Sun safe poster

Design a poster to inform people about sun safety.

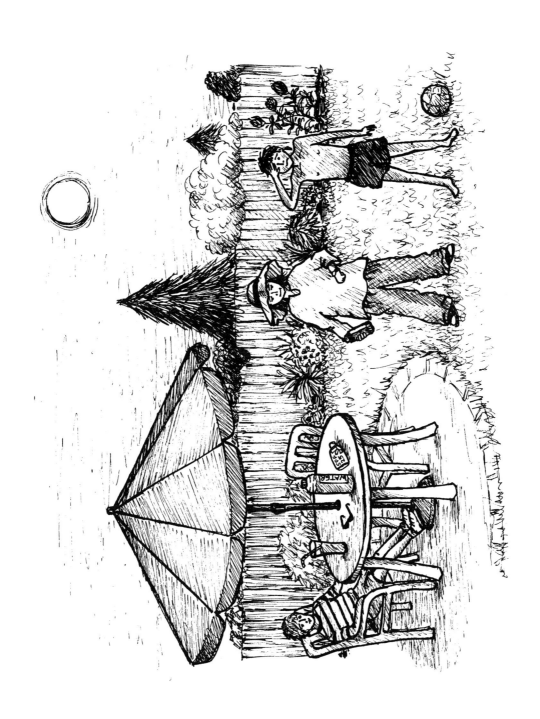

Response partners

Review your writing and then
ask a friend to do the same.
Write the comments in the speech bubbles.

What is the best part?

Which is your favourite character?

Which is your favourite line or sentence?

How could it be made better?

Self-assessment

How do you think you have done?

very good   OK   not so good

Writing activity:

Planning:

Writing style:

Layout:

Punctuation:

Special vocabulary:

Spelling:

Editing/redrafting:

Final published presentation:

Other comments:

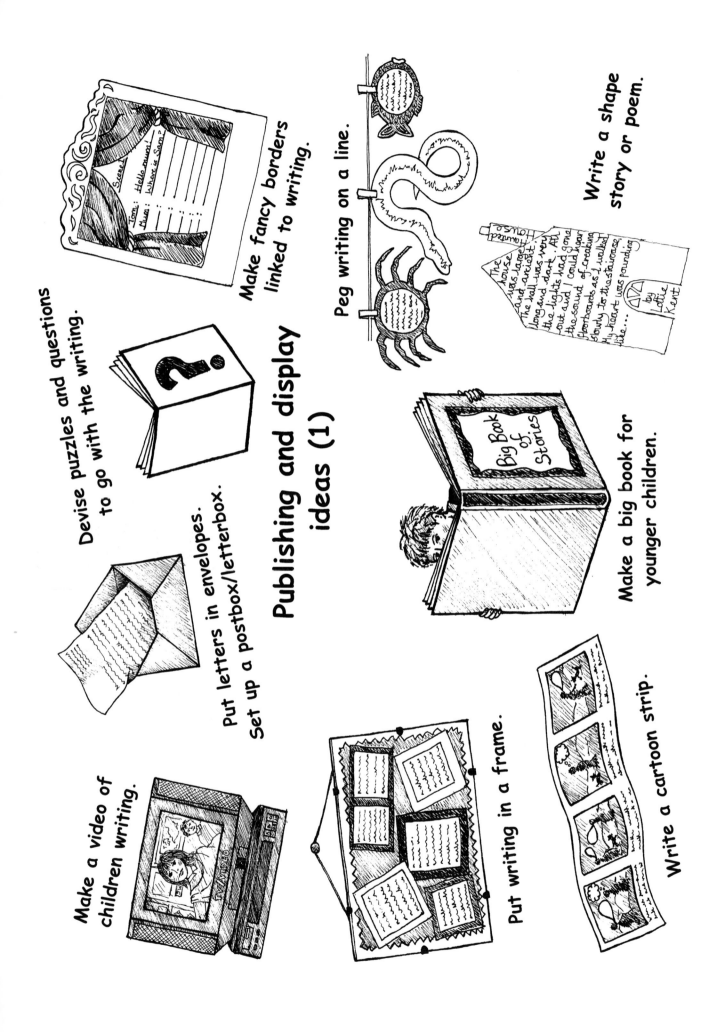

Publishing and display ideas (1)

Make fancy borders linked to writing.

Peg writing on a line.

Write a shape story or poem.

Devise puzzles and questions to go with the writing.

Make a big book for younger children.

Put letters in envelopes. Set up a postbox/letterbox.

Make a video of children writing.

Put writing in a frame.

Write a cartoon strip.

Publishing and display ideas (2)

Make a newspaper or magazine.

Put the writing on a 3-D shape.

Put writing on a wall mural.

Experiment with font style and layout on the computer.

Make an environment to display/contain the writing.

Put the words to a well-known tune.

Make scrolls.

Make a book with moving parts.

Put it on tape.

Writing targets

Three things I need to work on:

Writing targets

Three things I need to work on: